Within Word Pattern, Volume 2

Words Their Way

CLASSROOM

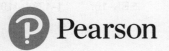

Pearson

Glenview, Illinois   Boston, Massachusetts
Chandler, Arizona   New York, New York

Photographs

Cover ARTIKAL/Shutterstock; eva_mask/Shutterstock; Morphart Creation/Shutterstock; olllikeballoon/Shutterstock; rolandtopor/Shutterstock; Nadezda Barkova/Shutterstock; Gregory Johnston/Alamy

Pearson Education, Inc. 330 Hudson Street, New York, NY 10013

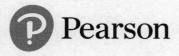

ISBN 13: 978-1-4284-4190-3
ISBN-10:   1-4284-4190-5

2   18

Contents

r-Influenced Vowel Patterns er, ear, eer

er	ear	eer	ear = ur
her	ear	deer	earn

Write on the lines words from your sort with the same vowel sound and pattern as her, ear, deer, and earn.

her	ear	deer	earn

Sort 25: r-Influenced Vowel Patterns er, ear, eer

r-Influenced Vowel Patterns ir, ire, ier

ir	ire	ier	oddball
bird	fire	drier	tire
third	girl	birth	their
flier	shirt	fir	wire
hire	pliers	crier	
frier	fur		

r-Influenced Vowel Patterns ir, ire, ier

ir	ire	ier	Oddball
bird	**fire**	**drier**	

Sort 26: r-Influenced Vowel Patterns ir, ire, ier

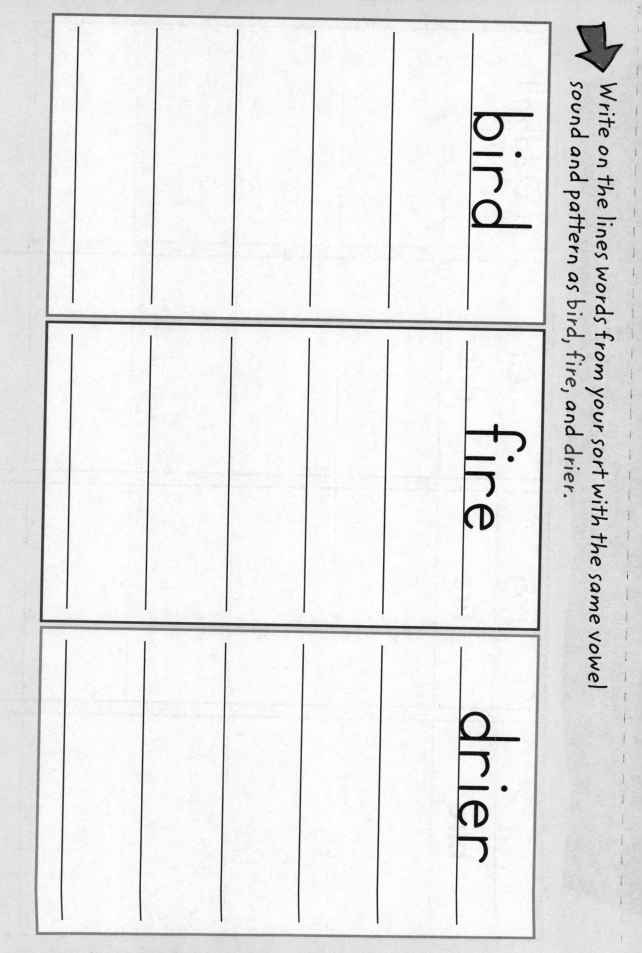

bird	fire	drier

r-Influenced Vowel Patterns

LVLS

ur	ure	ur-e
turn	sure	curve

Write on the lines from your sort with the same vowel sound and pattern as turn, sure, and curve.

turn	sure	curve

ar	ėr	or
	worm	fork

cure

| hard | score | earn | snore | nerve | pearl | worth | card | bore |
| yard | spur | horse | search | yarn | chore | bar | sharp | torn |

ar

ėr

or

oi	oy	
point	**boy**	broil
join	soil	soy
spoil	oil	coil
joy	coin	moist
joint	boil	toy

Diphthongs oi, oy

oy					
boy					

oi					
point					

p	s	b	c	j	t	n	l	sp	nt

oi

oy

would	stool	crook	spool	groom
spoon	could	troop	wood	foot	soot
nook	hook	root	hoop	tool	wool
fool	brook	hood	noon	should	stood

Vowel Digraph oo

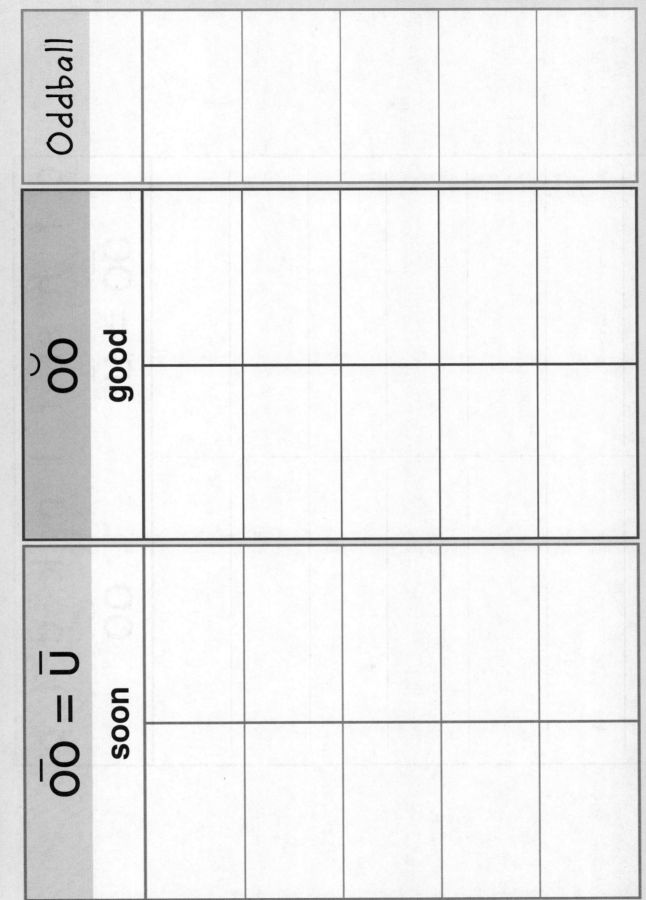

$\bar{oo} = \bar{U}$ soon	$\breve{oo}$ good	Oddball

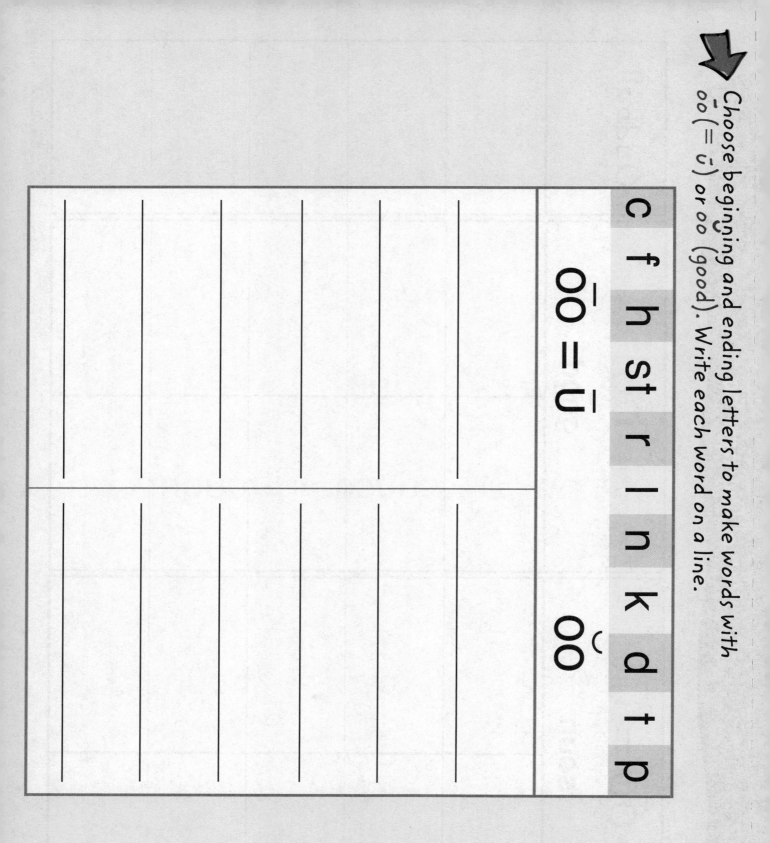

Choose beginning and ending letters to make words with
oo̅ (= u̅) or oŏ (good). Write each word on a line.

c f h st r l n k d t p

oo̅ = u̅   oŏ

aw	au	oddball
saw	**caught**	
lawn	cause	paw
straw	fault	law
claw	sauce	taught
draw	laugh	haul
pause	yawn	haunt
hawk	crawl	dawn
launch	vault	

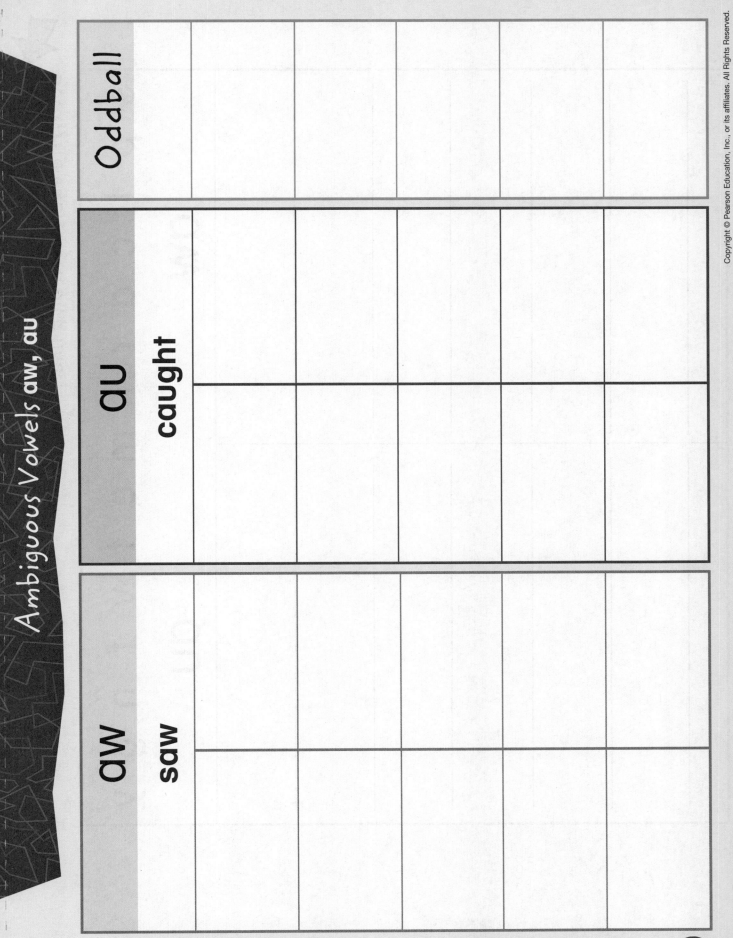

aw	au	Oddball
saw	**caught**	

s p l c d r h m e t v f n g y	
aw	**au**

wa	al	ough
watch	**small**	**thought**
walk	salt	wash
tall	bought	wand
almost	wasp	fought
swap	chalk	ought
swat	brought	cough
also		

wa	al	ough
watch	**small**	**thought**

| wash | almost | wand | small | brought | cough | thought | talk |
| bought | walk | ought | wasp | watch | also | tall | swap |

wa	al	ough

Diphthongs ou, ow

ground	south	mouth	pound
couch	frown	town	clown
drown	owl	howl	tough
plow	shout	growl	count
gown	scout	cloud	crown
	rough	found	grown

OU						OW						Oddball					
sound						brown											

t	h	n	l	s	cl	c	b	r	f	sc	d	g	p

ou

vowel

ow

sound

kn-	wr-	gn-	oddball
knife	wrong	gnat	
rap	knack	wreck	known
wrist	knot	gnaw	ring
wrap	knob	knit	wren
wring	knight	knoll	write
wreath	night	not	

kn-	wr-	gn-	Oddball
knife	wrong	gnat	

kn-	wr-	gn-
knife	wrong	gnat

scr-	str-	spr-
screen	**strong**	**spring**
stress	scrap	strict
straight	scream	string
scrape	spray	spruce
strange	scratch	stripe
stretch	sprout	scram
scribe	spread	script

spr- spring							

str- strong							

scr- screen							

Write on the lines words from your sort that begin with scr-, str-, and spr-.

scr-	str-	spr-

Sort 36: Triple r-Blends scr-, str-, spr-

thr-	shr-	squ-	spl-
three	shred	square	split
throne	through	shrunk	squeak
shrink	shrub	thrill	splotch
squint	squirm	squawk	throw
squeeze	splash	squish	shrimp
squash	shriek	threw	thrifty
shrewd	threat	shrug	splinter

spl-	squ-	shr-	thr-
split	**square**	**shred**	**three**

thr-	shr-	squ-	spl-

Sort 37: Triple Blends thr, shr, squ, spl

germ	cub	gym	coat
cent	corn	gem	cease
game	calf	guide	guess
goose	cart	cell	guest
	gist	golf	code

Hard and Soft c and g

soft c	hard c	soft g	hard g
city	card	giant	gave

Say each word. Write on the lines words from the box that have each c or g sound.

| cell | goose | gist | coat | calf | gym | cub | guest |
| golf | code | gem | cease | game | cent | guide | cart |

hard c

soft c

hard g

soft g

-ze	-se /s/	-se /z/	-ve	-ce
freeze	**house**	**please**	**move**	**chance**
choose	glove	leave	loose	sneeze
piece	geese	fence	snooze	dance
wise	peace	breeze	mouse	cheese
prove	bounce	chase	solve	rinse
twelve	glance	raise	sense	false
		sleeve	once	prize

-ce	-ve	-se /z/	se /s/	-ze
chance	move	please	house	freeze

Choose beginning and middle letters to make words with ending letters -ce, -ve, -se, and -ze. Write each word on a line. You will use some letters more than once.

ch	pr	p	m	gl	l	s	fr	pl	sn	o	an	i	ea	oo	ee	ie

-ce	-ve	-se	-ze

badge	charge	stage
rage	ridge	surge
range	judge	cage
huge	fudge	change
dodge	page	sponge
bridge	bulge	

-dge	-ge	r,l,n+ -ge
edge	**age**	**large**

Write on the lines words from your sort that end in -dge or -ge.

-dge	-ge
_____	_____
_____	_____
_____	_____
_____	_____
_____	_____
_____	_____
_____	_____
_____	_____
_____	_____

Sort 40: Word Endings -dge, -ge

witch	torch	peach
screech	gulch	pitch
coach	bench	sketch
which	fetch	branch
beach	rich	match
speech	much	crunch
hutch	teach	munch

Oddball	r,l,n+ -ch	-ch	-tch
	porch	reach	catch

Write on the lines words from your sort that end with -tch or -ch.

-tch	-ch
_____	_____
_____	_____
_____	_____
_____	_____
_____	_____
_____	_____
_____	_____
_____	_____
_____	_____

Sort 41: Word Endings -tch, -ch

a_e	ai	oddball
sale	plain	hair
there	waist	they're
fair	maid	main
pale	whale	tail
bail	their	hare
made	tale	sail
plane	wail	fare
bale	mane	stare
waste	stair	pail

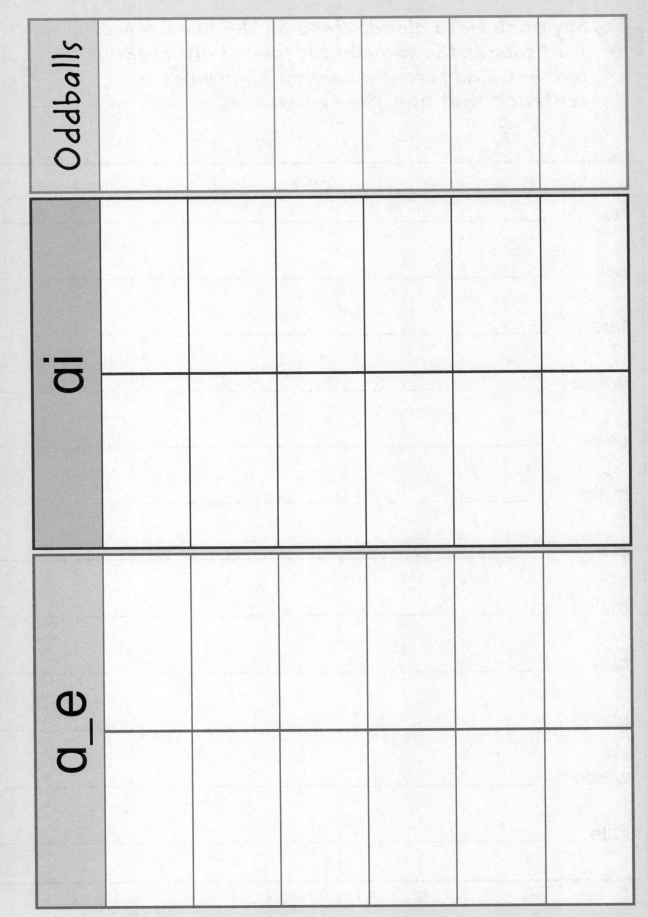

Oddballs	ai	a_e

Say each word aloud. Write on the line a word that sounds the same but is spelled differently and has a different meaning. Then write a sentence that uses the new word.

tale _____

sail _____

fare _____

whale _____

pale _____

main _____

stair _____

maid _____

hare _____

plain _____

waste _____

bale _____

Sort 42: Long a Homophones #1

a_e	ai	ea	ei
rein	reign	ate	vane
weight	pane	pair	wait
rain	wade	stake	pare
pain	brake	vein	
pear	steak	vain	
eight	break	weighed	

ei	ea	ai	a_e

Say each word aloud. Write on the line a word that sounds the same but is spelled differently and has a different meaning. Then write a sentence that uses the new word.

rein _____

stake _____

weighed _____

brake _____

weight _____

pane _____

vein _____

pare _____

ate _____

Sort 43: Long a Homophones #2

Sort 44

mist	in
dye	it's
missed	I
night	billed
fined	eye
write	him
side	hi
its	sighed
build	knight
die	find
right	inn
high	hymn

Short and Long i Homophones

Sort 44: Short and Long i Homophones

87

Say each word aloud. Write on the line a word that sounds the same but is spelled differently and has a different meaning. Then write a sentence that uses the new word.

missed _____

inn _____

die _____

its _____

eye _____

night _____

billed _____

fined _____

right _____

hymn _____

side _____

hi _____

Sort 44: Short and Long i Homophones

Long Vowel	Short Vowel	Other Vowels
tēar	lĭve	sōw
rēad	băss	woūnd
wĭnd	clōse	clōse
lēad	līve	wīnd
rĕad	bow	wound
bāss	teār	bōw
sow	lĕad	

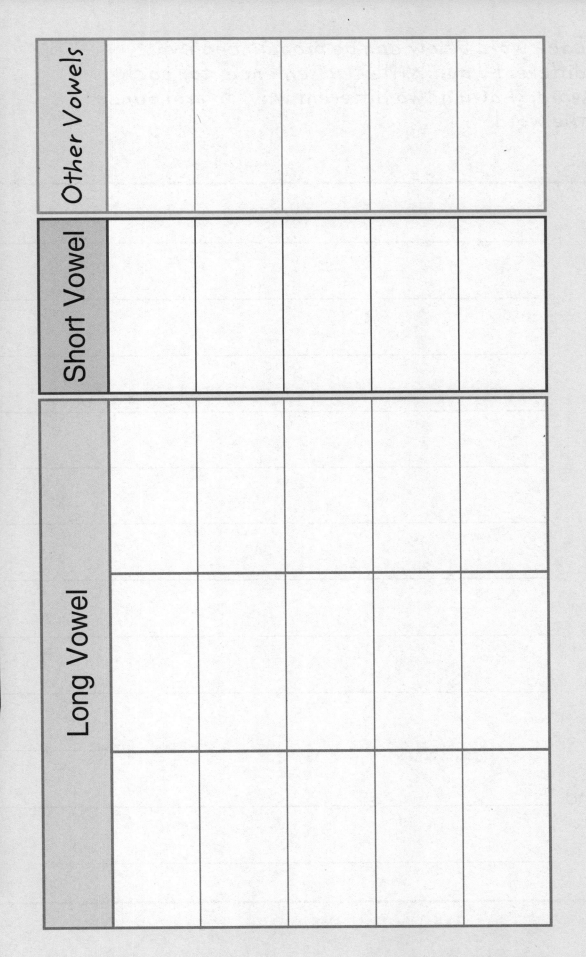

Long Vowel		Short Vowel	Other Vowels

Each word below can be pronounced two different ways. Write two sentences for each word, showing two different ways to pronounce the word.

bow
_____

_____

live
_____

_____

read
_____

_____

tear
_____

_____

wind
_____

_____

wound
_____

_____